Pebble® Plus

AFRICAN ANIMALS

Meerkats

by Jody Sullivan Rake
Consulting Editor: Gail Saunders-Smith, PhD

Consultant:
George Wittemyer, PhD
NSF International Postdoctoral Fellow
University of California at Berkeley

Capstone press®

Mankato, Minnesota

Pebble Plus is published by Capstone Press,
151 Good Counsel Drive, P.O. Box 669, Mankato, Minnesota 56002.
www.capstonepress.com

1 2 3 4 5 6 13 12 11 10 09 08

Library of Congress Cataloging-in-Publication Data
Rake, Jody Sullivan.
    Meerkats / by Jody Sullivan Rake.
    p. cm. — (Pebble plus. African animals)
    Includes bibliographical references and index.
    ISBN-13: 978-1-4296-1249-4 (hardcover)
    ISBN-10: 1-4296-1249-5 (hardcover)
    1. Meerkat — Africa — Juvenile literature. I. Title. II. Series.
QL737.C235R35 2008
599.74'2 — dc22   2007028679

Summary: Discusses meerkats, their African habitat, food, and behavior.

Editorial Credits
Erika L. Shores, editor; Renée T. Doyle, designer; Laura Manthe, photo researcher

Photo Credits
Afripics.com, 14–15, 18–19
Art Life Images/David Paynter, 12–13
Bruce Coleman Inc./Clem Haagner, 20–21
iStockphoto/Jacynth Roode, cover; Nico Smit, 8–9; Peter Malsbury, 1; xyno, 22
Shutterstock/EcoPrint, 6–7, 16–17; Nicola Gavin, cover, 1, 3 (fur), 10–11
SuperStock Inc./ZSSD, 4–5

Note to Parents and Teachers

The African Animals set supports national science standards related to life science.
This book describes and illustrates meerkats. The images support early readers in
understanding the text. The repetition of words and phrases helps early readers learn
new words. This book also introduces early readers to subject-specific vocabulary words,
which are defined in the Glossary section. Early readers may need assistance to read
some words and to use the Table of Contents, Glossary, Read More, Internet Sites, and
Index sections of the book.

Table of Contents

Living in Africa

Meerkats live in Africa.

They play in the sun.

They rest in the shade.

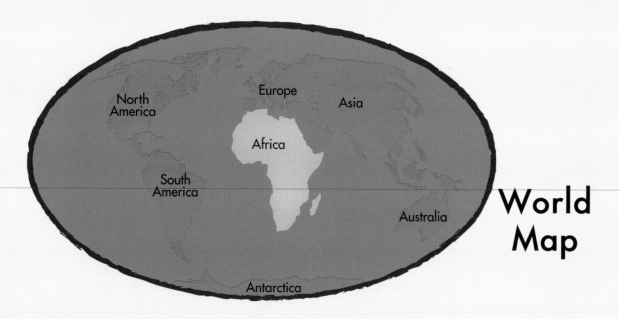

North America

Europe

Asia

Africa

South America

Australia

Antarctica

World Map

4

Some meerkats live on
grassy savannas.
Other meerkats live on
dry plains.

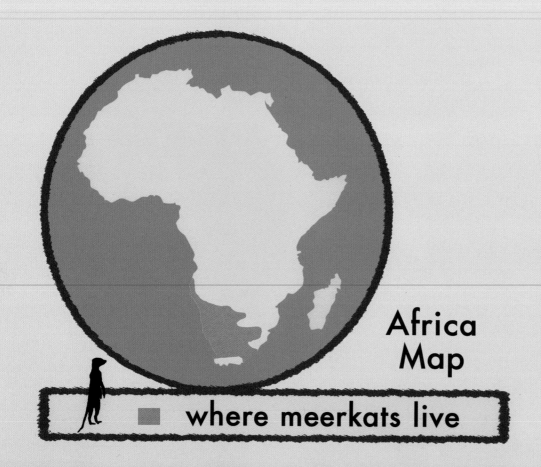

Africa
Map

where meerkats live

Up Close!

Meerkats stand up straight
on their hind legs.
They look for danger
all around.

Meerkats use sharp claws
to dig burrows.
They also dig for food.

Eating

Meerkats eat bugs, reptiles, and small rodents.

What a creepy crawly meal!

Water is often hard to find

where meerkats live.

They get water

from the food they eat.

Staying Safe

There is safety in numbers.

Meerkats live together

in mobs.

One meerkat stays behind
while the mob hunts.
The meerkat babysitter
watches over the pups.

Meerkats bark to warn

the mob of predators.

Meerkats run to their burrows

to hide underground.

Stay safe, meerkats!

Glossary

burrow — a tunnel or hole in the ground made or used by an animal

mob — a group of meerkats that live together

plains — open land with few trees

predator — an animal that hunts other animals for food; eagles and jackals hunt meerkats.

pup — a young meerkat

reptile — a cold-blooded animal that breathes air and has a backbone; most reptiles have scaly skin.

rodent — a small mammal with long front teeth

savanna — a flat, grassy plain with few trees

Read More

Ciovacco, Justine. *Meerkats.* All about Animals. Pleasantville, N.Y.: Reader's Digest Young Families, 2007.

Lunde, Darrin P. *Meet the Meerkat.* Watertown, Mass.: Charlesbridge, 2007.

Storad, Conrad J. *Meerkats.* Early Bird Nature Books. Minneapolis: Lerner, 2007.

Internet Sites

FactHound offers a safe, fun way to find Internet sites related to this book. All of the sites on FactHound have been researched by our staff.

Here's how:

1. Visit *www.facthound.com*

2. Choose your grade level.

3. Type in this book ID **1429612495** for age-appropriate sites. You may also browse subjects by clicking on letters, or by clicking on pictures and words.

4. Click on the **Fetch It** button.

FactHound will fetch the best sites for you!

Index

Word Count: 125
Grade: 1
Early-Intervention Level: 16